Wow! Erie Tribes!

Written by Elke Sündermann

Copyright ©2012 by Elke Sündermann
All rights reserved. No part of this book* may be reproduced or transmitted in any form or by any means without written permission of the author.
*Permission is granted to copy, distribute and/or modify the photos in this document under the terms of the GNU Free Documentation License, Version 1.3 or any later version published by the Free Software Foundation; with no Invariant Sections.

This book includes  icons to help you stop, think, and discuss what you just read. These can be used to ask yourself a question about what you just read. If you can't, then read it again!

1

Regions of U.S. Native Americans

Native American History

Have you ever wondered what the U.S. was like long ago? Native Americans were the first people to live here!

There are many tribes of Native Americans. Depending on where they lived, their food, shelter, clothing, and language were different.

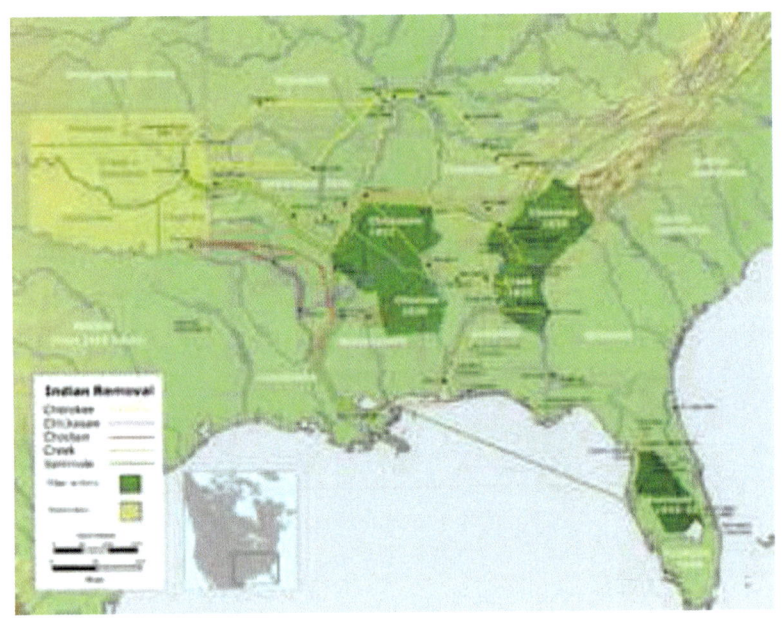

Cherokee Trail of Tears

Things changed a lot when the settlers came to the United States. Some of their greetings were peaceful, and some were not.

Many natives died, from battles and diseases. The U.S. army moved many natives away from their homes, like the Cherokee in the Trail of Tears.

Honey bee carrying pollen

They had to learn to live off the new land. These areas are called **"reservations."**

They taught the settlers many things, like how to grow corn, squash, beans, and peanuts.

The settlers also learned how to raise turkeys and bees for food, and how to grow cotton.

Modern Native Americans

Some Native Americans today live with their tribes on reservations like they did hundreds of years ago. Others have modern lives in towns. Their **culture** is strong, adding **diversity** to our world. We'll read about Shawnee tribes and how they lived. **What Do You Know?**

- List 3 things that Native Americans taught the settlers.

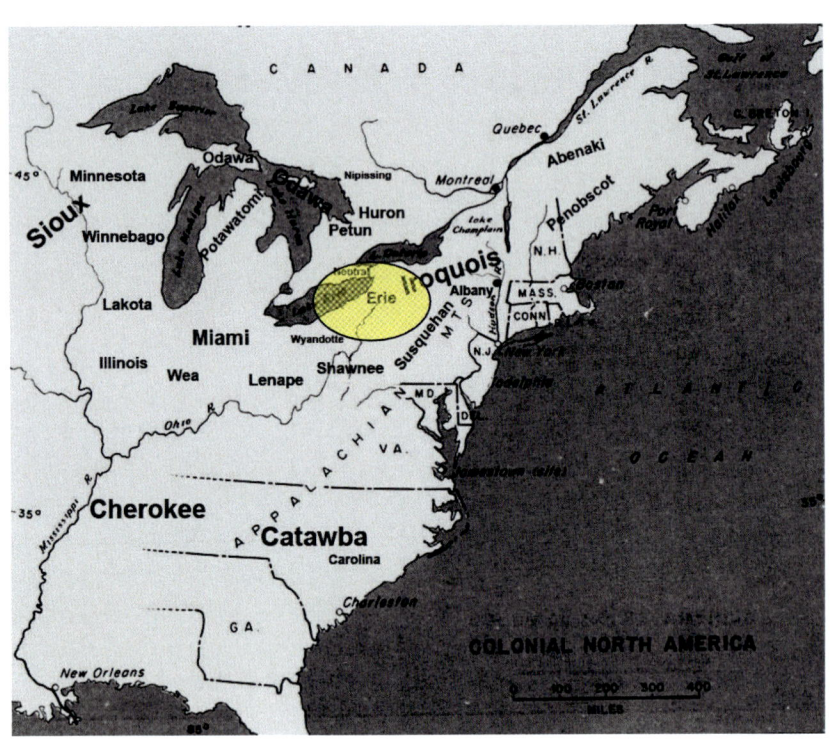

Erie tribe territory

Erie Native Americans

The Erie tribes lived south of Lake Erie, in the area now known as Ohio, New York, and Pennsylvania.

The name Erie means "long tail," after the raccoons and big cats that roamed their area (possibly mountain lions, pumas, or panthers.) They were also called Cat people and Raccoon people.

Palisade built around a village

The Erie spoke a **dialect** of the Iroquois language. We believe they lived in small villages, in long houses for many families to live in. They protected their villages with wooden **palisade** walls.

They were sedentary (didn't move from place to place), so they grew gardens (mostly corn, beans, and squash, called the Three Sisters.)

Planting Three Sisters on 2009

Native American dollar coin

Many tribes grew the Three sisters, so that the beans climbed up the corn and put minerals in the ground, while the squash on the ground kept weeds away. In the winters, they ate from stored crops, and they hunted. It is thought they also weaved mats and made pottery for cooking.

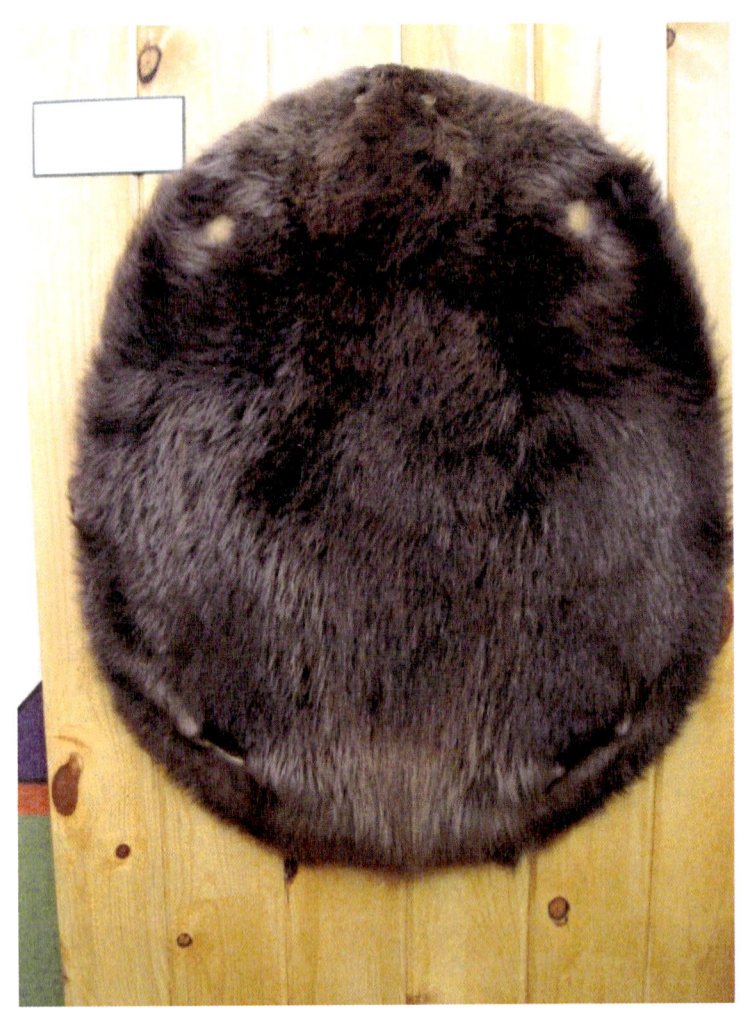

Beaver pelt for fur trade

The Erie tribe helped Huron tribe **refugees** against the Iroquois tribes. The Erie hunted beaver to trade, and when they blocked the Ohio hunting grounds from the Iroquois, they went to war. There were around 15,000 Erie, but without firearms they lost and were **absorbed** by the Seneca (part of the Iroquois.) Some Seneca today claim to be Erie **descendants**.

Archaeologists looking for

clues to history

The Erie were great warriors (they may have used poison-tipped arrows), but the last group of Erie surrendered to the Iroquois in the 1600s, although it's possible they fled west.

Scientists believe the Erie tribes are descendants of ancient mound-building cultures, and probably wore animal furs and skins.

Some believe that they became the Shawnee tribe, or that they moved south. Some think they went north. We're not really sure what happened to them.

How will you leave your mark on our world?

Erie Snapshot					
Region	Tribe name	Food	Shelter	Clothing	Other facts
Midwest, Lake Erie	Erie	Hunted, three sisters	Wood longhouse	Animal fur and hides	Poison arrows, disappeared?

What can you do on Erie land now?

- Take a tour and check out the artifacts and new exhibits at the Indian Museum of Lake County, OH
- Find out more about how we know about the Erie at the New Indian Ridge Museum – Amherst, OH
- Archeological sites where many artifacts have been found:

- Welling Site – Coshocton County
- Paleo Crossing – Medina County
- Serpent Mound – Adams County

Glossary

Absorbed – to assimilate, or be taken into another group.

Archaeologist – a person who studies past life and cultures

Trail of Tears – after the Indian removal act in 1830, five tribes were moved off their land (Cherokee were moved in 1838.) 46,000 Native

Americans were removed to open 25 million acres of land for settlement.

Culture – group with similar beliefs and behaviors

Descendants – a person who is related by generations to an ancestor

Dialects – different varieties of the same language, spoken by a group of people

Diversity – variety and differences

Firearms – a small **arms** weapon that **fires** something out of it with gunpowder

Govern – to control or rule a place or people and their behaviors

Nation – a large group of people organized under a single government

Nomads – people who have no permanent home, who move from place to place for food, water, and land

Palisade – a barrier fence of wood, or line of cliffs, used for defense

Region – a large area of land

Refugees – people who flee for safety, and taken in by another group

Reservation – a piece of land set apart by the government for the use of Native Americans

References

All information in this book comes from Wikipedia, Facts for Kids, Yahoo Kids Dictionary Search websites, and from several years of teaching this unit of learning with miscellaneous materials and sources. Photos credited to Wikimedia Commons.

Made in the USA
Middletown, DE
09 January 2025

69171684R00015